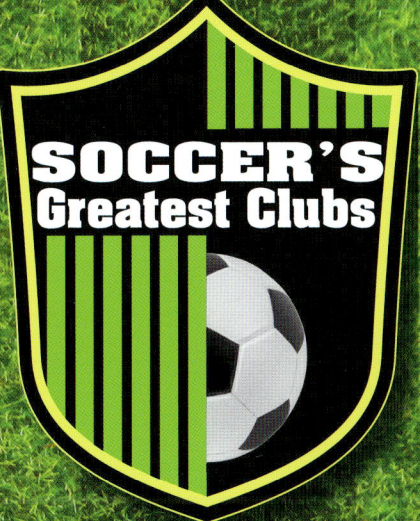

FC Bayern Munich

Derek Miller

New York

Published in 2020 by Cavendish Square Publishing, LLC
243 5th Avenue, Suite 136, New York, NY 10016

Copyright © 2020 by Cavendish Square Publishing, LLC

First Edition

No part of this publication may be reproduced, stored in a retrieval system, or transmitted in any form or by any means—electronic, mechanical, photocopying, recording, or otherwise—without the prior permission of the copyright owner. Request for permission should be addressed to Permissions, Cavendish Square Publishing, 243 5th Avenue, Suite 136, New York, NY 10016. Tel (877) 980-4450; fax (877) 980-4454.

Website: cavendishsq.com

This publication represents the opinions and views of the author based on his or her personal experience, knowledge, and research. The information in this book serves as a general guide only. The author and publisher have used their best efforts in preparing this book and disclaim liability rising directly or indirectly from the use and application of this book.

All websites were available and accurate when this book was sent to press.

Library of Congress Cataloging-in-Publication Data

Names: Miller, Derek L., author.
Title: FC Bayern Munich / Derek Miller.
Description: First edition. | New York : Cavendish Square, 2020. | Series: Soccer's greatest clubs | Includes bibliographical references and index. | Audience: Grade 5 to 8.
Identifiers: LCCN 2019020778 (print) | LCCN 2019021841 (ebook) | ISBN 9781502652775 (library bound) | ISBN 9781502652768 (pbk.)
Subjects: LCSH: FC Bayern (Soccer team)--History--Juvenile literature. | Soccer teams--Germany--Munich--Juvenile literature.
Classification: LCC GV943.6.F36 M55 2020 (print) | LCC GV943.6.F36 (ebook) | DDC 796.334/640943364--dc23
LC record available at https://lccn.loc.gov/2019020778
LC ebook record available at https://lccn.loc.gov/2019021841

Editor: Kristen Susienka
Copy Editor: Rebecca Rohan
Associate Art Director: Alan Sliwinski
Designer: Joe Parenteau
Production Coordinator: Karol Szymczuk
Photo Research: J8 Media

The photographs in this book are used by permission and through the courtesy of: Cover Christian Kaspar-Barke/Bongarts/Getty Images; p. 1 (and used throughout) Soccer ball - Focus Stocker/Shutterstock.com, Emblem - Onur Cem/Shutterstock.com, Grass - Comzeal Images/Shutterstock.com; p. 4 Adam Pretty/Bongarts/Getty Images; p. 6 Wikimedia Commons/File:Bayern munich 1900.jpg/Public Domain; p. 7 Charnsitr/Shutterstock.com; p. 8 Matthew Ashton/EMPICS/Getty Images, p. 9 Gabriel Bouys/AFP/Getty Images, p. 12 Rust/Ullstein Image/Getty Images; p. 14 Rainer Lesniewski/Shutterstock.com; p. 17 Christof Stache/AFP/Getty Images; p. 22 Joch/Ullstein Picture/Getty Images; p. 25 Popperfoto/Getty Images; p. 26 Friedemann Vogel/Bongarts/Getty Images; p. 29 Lars Baron/Bongarts/Getty Images; pp. 31, 33 Alexander Hassenstein/Bongarts/Getty Images; p. 34 David Ramos/Getty Images; p. 36 Johannes Simon/Bongarts/Getty Images; p. 41 Taranchic/Shutterstock.com; p. 43 Martin Rose/Bongarts/Getty Images; p. 45 Sampics/Corbis/Getty Images; p. 47 Andreas Gebert/Picture Alliance/Getty Images; p. 48 Andrew Surma/NurPhoto/Getty Images; p. 50 TF-Images/Getty Images; p. 51 Stefan Matzke - Sampics/Corbis/Getty Images; p. 52 Stuart Franklin/Bongarts/Getty Images; p. 54 Michael Reaves/Getty Images.

Printed in the United States of America

TABLE OF CONTENTS

Chapter 1:
The Club That Dominates 5

Chapter 2:
A Tradition of Excellence 13

Chapter 3:
Awards and Championships 27

Chapter 4:
Overcoming Challenges 37

Chapter 5:
The Future of Bayern 49

Chronology 55
Glossary 56
Further Information 58
Selected Bibliography 60
Index 62
About the Author 64

Team captain Manuel Neuer (*center*) holds the German Super Cup trophy as Bayern celebrates their 2018 victory.

THE CLUB THAT DOMINATES

FC Bayern Munich (also called Bayern or Bayern Munich) is a powerhouse of professional soccer. It is the most successful club in Germany, where it dominates the national league. On the world stage, Bayern competes at the highest level. Few clubs can match its record of excellence and the large number of championship titles it has won.

HUMBLE BEGINNINGS

Bayern was founded in 1900. At the time, there was little reason to think it would become a world-famous club. It was created by a group of players in the city of Munich. They wanted to play against other local teams. Soccer was just starting to become popular in Germany back then. The first soccer game in Germany had taken place in 1874. The game's rules weren't formalized until later. In 1900, some teams played with an oval ball instead of a round ball. An oval ball had been used to play a game that was popular before soccer. It combined rules of rugby and soccer. Eventually, that game became

SPORT SHORT
When FC Bayern Munich was founded, Germany was ruled by an emperor. His name was Kaiser Wilhelm II.

two separate games, which we now know as rugby and soccer.

Bayern was just one team of many in Munich. At first, its fans didn't even have stands, or sections with seating, to sit in. The club had to partner with another club, Münchner Sportclub. Bayern had little money, and there were few playing fields in the city. While Bayern stayed an independent team, the club agreed to wear the red and white colors of Münchner Sportclub. Today, Bayern still wears red and white as its official colors, as well as blue.

Over time, Bayern began to stand out. It became the best team in Munich, then it became the

In the early 1900s, Bayern players wore white jerseys.

The white and blue pattern in the center of Bayern's logo is taken from the flag of the team's home state, Bavaria.

best team in Germany, and finally it became the best team across all of Europe. Today, Bayern has more fans than any other German club. There are 4,400 official fan clubs across the globe and a total of 352,000 registered members.

THE BUNDESLIGA

Bayern took the lead in German soccer through its success in the Bundesliga. The Bundesliga is the

SPORT SHORT

In 1900, seventeen soccer players met at a restaurant in Munich. Led by a man named Franz Josef, they signed a document that created FC Bayern Munich. One hundred and twenty years later, FC Bayern Munich is a popular team in Germany and around the world.

The Club That Dominates 7

professional soccer league in Germany. It was founded in 1963. Since then, German clubs have competed each year to win the Bundesliga title. The winner is crowned German soccer champion.

Bayern won its first title in the 1968–1969 Bundesliga season. Over the years, Bayern has outplayed all other German teams. Throughout the history of the Bundesliga, Bayern has brought home the title almost half the time. This is far more than any other team.

Bayern's success in the Bundesliga led to its reputation as the best German team in modern times. Not many other German soccer clubs have been able to challenge Bayern on the field. To find teams of equal skill, Bayern often has to look to clubs outside of Germany.

THE UEFA CHAMPIONS LEAGUE

The Union of European Football Association's (UEFA) Champions League is a competition that pits the top European soccer clubs against each other. The top thirty-two teams from around Europe face off. The winner takes home the European Champions Clubs' Cup. It is one of the most prestigious trophies in the sport. Many of the best teams in the world, like Real Madrid and AC Milan, battle to win.

The European Champions Clubs' Cup is on display here.

Bayern has an impressive record in the UEFA Champions League. It has won the title five times and placed second five times as of 2019. Bayern's most recent victory in the UEFA Champions League was in 2013. They defeated Borussia Dortmund, a rival from the Bundesliga, 2–1.

THE GERMAN NATIONAL TEAM

Clubs like Bayern do not compete in some international tournaments like the World Cup or the summer Olympics. Instead, the best players from many teams play for their home country on a national team. Since clubs like Bayern have players from many

Bayern player Mario Götze (in white) scored the winning goal of the 2014 FIFA World Cup for the German national team.

The Club That Dominates 9

SPORT SHORT

In 1910, a Bayern Munich player joined the German national team for the first time.

different countries, teammates may even face off in these tournaments.

Unsurprisingly, the German national team owes a great deal to Bayern. Bayern is Germany's most successful club. Just over half of Bayern's players are Germans. This means the ability of the German national team often rises and falls with Bayern's.

Today, about one-third of the German national team is made up of Bayern players. In 2014, the German national team won the World Cup final in Brazil 1–0. Bayern player Mario Götze scored the only goal of the game in overtime. He was just twenty-two years old. This made Götze the youngest player to score in a World Cup final since 1966.

CLUB VALUES

Bayern's success has not weakened the values it was founded on. The team holds itself to a high standard. It has key values that guide it on and off the field: tradition, responsibility, respect, family, confidence, innovation, financial responsibility, partnership, joy, its role as a club, and the importance of its players being role models.

Bayern tries to be a successful business that manages its money well. Just as importantly, the club wants to be fair in all its dealings. The club treats fans, team members, and opponents with respect. Bayern focuses on the real purpose of sport: taking joy in the game.

The values of Bayern have guided the club throughout its history. The team has stood against racism and anti-Semitism. Anti-Semitism is prejudice against Jewish people. Even during Germany's darkest times under Adolf Hitler and the Nazi Party, Bayern turned its back on hatred. Today, the club opens its arms to people from other countries looking for safety in Germany.

Bayern legends Gerd Mueller (*left*) and Uli Hoeness (*right*) helped carry the team to greatness in the 1970s.

A TRADITION OF EXCELLENCE

Over its 120-year history, Bayern has seen many triumphs and setbacks. Today, the club is at the top of its game. However, the road to this point was not always easy. Bayern overcame many challenges to become the most successful club in Germany.

THE EARLY YEARS

Seventeen soccer players started Bayern in 1900. At this early date in the sport's history, Bayern was just one of many local clubs in Munich. The city of Munich was—and remains—the third largest city in Germany. At the time of its founding, there was no telling Bayern would lead German soccer.

In 1910, Bayern won its first title in Munich's Eastern District league. It was an early success but still a very local one. By 1920, Bayern had become the club with the largest number of fans in Munich, yet they faced stiff competition from other clubs. It was only in 1926 that Bayern finally won the South German Championship. The championship included teams in Munich and neighboring cities in southern Germany. By

A Tradition of Excellence   13

that time, Bayern's rival FC Nürnberg had already won the South German Championship on four occasions. Bayern was a rising star. Still, it was not the clear leader it is today.

A UNIQUE CULTURE

Like FC Nürnberg, Bayern Munich calls the German state of Bavaria home. Bavaria—and its largest city, Munich—have a culture that is unique from the rest of Germany. In the past, Bavarians wore their own traditional clothes. Today, their way of speaking is still different from the German spoken in the north of the country. The world-famous German festival of Oktoberfest started in Munich. It remains more popular in Munich than in the rest of the country.

Bavaria and its special traditions are held dear by Bayern fans. In fact, the word "Bayern" is the German word for "Bavaria." In German, the club is called

Bavaria is a large and important state in the southeast corner of Germany, as shown on this map.

14 FC Bayern Munich

1860 MUNICH: A LOCAL RIVAL

Local rivalries are often the most deeply felt. The history of Bayern is no exception. In the early days, there were many soccer teams from Munich. The two top teams were 1860 Munich and Bayern Munich. Depending on the year, they traded places as the top team in the city.

In 1963, the rivalry heated up with the creation of the national Bundesliga. The organizers of the Bundesliga did not want two teams from any one city to be in the top league. That year, 1860 was picked over Bayern. Although Bayern was allowed to join two years later, fans did not forget the insult. To make matters worse, the year that Bayern joined the top league, the team finished third, and 1860 took home the title.

Soon, Bayern entered its golden age in the 1970s, and 1860 faced a period of decline and was eventually downgraded to lower leagues. The two teams don't play each other anymore, but their fans are still fiercely divided.

"Fußball-Club Bayern München." This name is only half-translated to English. While "München" is translated to "Munich," "Bayern" is left as the German word for Bavaria.

NATIONAL CHAMPIONSHIP AND AN EMERGING THREAT

From 1919 to 1933, Bayern was led by club president Kurt Landauer. Landauer's decisions drove the club to stardom. The club recruited promising young players and trained them to become stars. This tradition is still followed today. Landauer focused on recruiting a highly skilled team rather than building a stadium like many fans wanted. His efforts paid off. In 1932, Bayern won its first national title. Recognized as the best team in Germany that year, it seemed like Bayern was going to be a top German team for many years to come.

Then, in 1933, Bayern's successes came to an end. A new political party, the Nazi Party, took power in Germany. Soon, the country changed from a democracy to a dictatorship led by Adolf Hitler. Hitler's racist ideas resulted in the persecution of Germany's Jewish population. Anti-Semitism became official state policy.

Landauer, a German Jewish man, chose to resign for the good of the club, as Jewish people were removed from important jobs around Germany. Bayern Munich was still regarded as a "Jewish club" anyway. Two of the seventeen founding members were Jewish, and some of its past coaches were Jewish. Bayern, like other organizations with any link to German Jewish people, was singled out for persecution. The team kept playing, but it lost money and fans. While the Nazis were in power between 1933 and 1945, Bayern struggled.

WORLD WAR II

In 1939, Nazi Germany invaded the neighboring country of Poland. This sparked World War II, which lasted until 1945. The war devastated countries around the world and led to the deaths of approximately eighty million people. Fifty-seven Bayern members died in the fighting.

Off the battlefield, at least fifteen million people were murdered by the Nazis, according to some historians. Jewish people, members of the LGBT+ community, and political opponents were imprisoned or executed without trial. Six million of the dead were Jewish people—about two-thirds of all the Jewish people in Europe at the time. This genocide, or attempt to kill an entire group of people, is called the Holocaust. Seven members of Bayern Munich were murdered by the Nazi government.

In 1938, Kurt Landauer was arrested because of his Jewish heritage and sent to Dachau concentration camp. Concentration camps housed prisoners in horrible conditions. Many died from diseases and the cold after being starved. Luckily, it was

Bayern Munich president Kurt Landauer was persecuted because of his Jewish heritage.

A Tradition of Excellence 17

discovered that Landauer was a decorated German war veteran. After thirty-three days in the concentration camp, he was released. Landauer fled to the country of Switzerland, leaving behind his beloved team in Munich.

Years later, Bayern traveled to Switzerland to play a game. It was during World War II, and the Gestapo—the Nazi police that terrorized Europe at the time—warned the team not to meet with Landauer. The team didn't dare defy the order. However, during the game, players saw Landauer watching from the stands. The team lined up on the field facing their former club president and applauded the man who had led them successfully for so many years before being forced to flee Germany. It was one of the most significant acts of defiance by a soccer club during Nazi rule.

When World War II ended in 1945 with Nazi Germany's defeat, Landauer returned to the country. It was a choice few German Jewish people made after the war. The crimes of the Nazi government were almost unimaginable and very personal. Four of Landauer's siblings had been murdered in the Holocaust.

Bayern welcomed back its former president with open arms. Landauer became president once again, and he ran the club until 1951. Bayern's history is tied tightly to his time as president. The club's defiance of the Gestapo in Switzerland is now a point of pride.

SPORT SHORT
Because of their red jerseys, Bayern Munich is known as "Die Roten," or "The Reds."

THE POSTWAR YEARS

The Nazi restrictions on soccer lifted after the war. Government-sponsored anti-Semitism was over. This change was a huge step forward for German soccer, but the war had devastated the country. Most cities were left in ruin, and money was scarce. What had once been Germany was now two countries: West Germany and East Germany. West Germany became a democracy and an ally of the United States. East Germany was a country very closely influenced by the Soviet Union. The Soviet Union was a communist country that faced off against the United States after World War II.

Munich was lucky enough to be in democratic West Germany, yet German soccer was left in chaos. East Germany and West Germany had their own leagues. In addition, German teams were largely amateur, or nonprofessional. Skilled players were drawn to professional teams in other countries. Bayern struggled to make a name for itself in the postwar German league.

In 1957, Bayern took home the German Cup (or DFB-Pokal) for the first time. The German Cup sees the top sixty-four German teams play against each other in a knockout cup competition. When a team loses, they are eliminated. The German Cup is different from the national championship that Bayern won in 1932 or the Bundesliga championships of later years.

Despite its success in the German Cup, Bayern had not yet recovered from its long decline during Nazi rule. The team won few other important victories in the years between the end of World War II and the start of the Bundesliga in 1963. The Bundesliga brought together teams from East and West Germany to play in the same league once again. However, when teams were picked for the new Bundesliga, Bayern's rival 1860 Munich was chosen to represent the city of Munich.

Left out of the new national league, Bayern turned its attention to finding new players to train. The club hoped their young recruits would become stars. Without much money, the club used Munich natives rather than international players to form the team. The team found and trained many new German soccer stars. Three of their top players during this time were Franz Beckenbauer, Gerd Müller, and Sepp Maier.

MAKING A WORLD-CLASS TEAM

Beckenbauer, Müller, and Maier joined the team in the 1960s. All three were from Bavaria. None of them had made a name for themselves yet. Beckenbauer and Maier first played for Bayern's youth team before joining the club. The youth league's ability to train talented local players and turn them into stars was—and is—an important advantage for Bayern.

Munich-born Beckenbauer joined Bayern in 1964, the same year the team was promoted to the Bundesliga. He played the position of defender, preventing the other team from scoring goals. However, Beckenbauer played the position quite offensively. Given the opportunity, he would attack and score against the opposing team. His style of play helped invent the position of sweeper—a defender who attacks and tries to score.

THE EMPEROR

Franz Beckenbauer's career did not end when he left Bayern in 1977. He went to the United States and played for the New York Cosmos. Three of the four years he played for the Cosmos, he helped the team win the Soccer Bowl. The Soccer Bowl is the North American soccer championship.

Beckenbauer also played for the German national team and helped carry them to greatness. He was on the field when West Germany won the World Cup in 1974. After retiring as a player, he was manager when the national team won the World Cup again in 1990.

Early in his career, Beckenbauer earned the nickname "the Emperor" ("Der Kaiser" in German). It is a fitting nickname for a player who is widely regarded as one of the best of all time. Throughout his distinguished career, Beckenbauer never forgot Bayern. It was the first team he played for, and Munich was his hometown. In the 1990s, he managed Bayern before becoming club president from 1994 to 2009.

From 1970 to 1977, Beckenbauer served as team captain for Bayern. He led the team to many victories in Germany and against clubs outside the country. Few players have been as influential in Bayern's history as Beckenbauer.

Müller was a striker who joined Bayern the same year as Beckenbauer. His ability to score goals was legendary. It earned him the nickname "Der Bomber," or "the Bomber" in English. Bayern's offensive game in the 1960s and 1970s depended on Müller's talent.

In lists of the best goal-scorers in soccer history, Müller ranks near the top. In 1972, the Bomber scored a record eighty-five goals in a single year. It was not until 2012 that his record was broken by Lionel Messi. Messi scored ninety-one goals.

Sepp Maier joined Bayern in 1962 after playing for the club's youth team for a few years. He would not leave the team until 1980. During that time, Maier's exceptional skill as goalie helped Bayern succeed. He earned the nickname "the Cat from Anzing" (his hometown in Bavaria) for his amazing reflexes and speed.

Today, Maier is regarded as one of the best goalkeepers in soccer

Gerd Müller (*left*), Franz Beckenbauer (*center*), and Sepp Maier (*right*) helped make Bayern a world-class team.

22 FC Bayern Munich

history. Unlike most other players, he only played for one club: Bayern. He still holds the record for playing the most Bayern matches in a row: 422.

BAYERN'S AMAZING RUN

With Beckenbauer, Müller, and Maier, Bayern became an unstoppable force in the late 1960s and 1970s. In 1968, the team won its first title in the Bundesliga. It was clear that Bayern was once again a top team in Germany.

   In the following years, Bayern would set a number of records. Players took home trophy after trophy. They won three back-to-back Bundesliga titles between 1972 and 1974. Even more astonishingly, Bayern began to dominate the UEFA Champions League (then called the European Cup). In 1974, 1975, and 1976, Bayern beat every other club across Europe. As a result, Bayern was crowned champions of the league three years in a row.

A GERMAN INSTITUTION

Since the 1970s, Bayern has continued to find success in the Bundesliga and in the UEFA Champions League. They have secured their place as one of the best clubs in the world. Beckenbauer, Maier, and Müller eventually left the team or retired. Luckily, they were replaced by new players who followed in their footsteps.

   The 1990s were a trying time for the club. They were defeated in the last seconds of the final match of the UEFA Champions League championship in 1999, after leading most of the game. Additionally, Bayern only won the Bundesliga's championship game three

SPORT SHORT

Germany has four World Cup–winning captains in its history, from the team's victories in 1954, 1974, 1990, and 2014. Three of those four captains played for FC Bayern Munich.

times in the 1990s. For any other team, this would have been great. For Bayern, it was not what they wanted or expected.

At the same time, Bayern earned the nickname "FC Hollywood" for its continuous attention in German newspapers. With their poor performance on the field, club members gave the press less-than-complimentary statements about one another. However, even in this dark period, Bayern was still a good team. In the 2000s, it would return to its former glory.

A NEW MILLENNIUM

In 2001, Bayern finally won the UEFA Champions League championship again. This was the first time the club had won in twenty-four years. This was followed by numerous Bundesliga titles. The Reds seemed untouchable. Few clubs could challenge them.

In 2006, Germany won the World Cup. Four Bayern players were on the German national team. This victory was a turning point for the Bundesliga, according to Beckenbauer. Speaking to *Sports Illustrated* in 2014, he said:

> *The big change was 2006, not only for Bayern but for the rest of the league.*

Bayern Munich players pose after winning the Champions League in 2001.

> *They get new stadiums and rebuild the stadiums. Then from this moment you have a lot better possibilities. You have more money for the players.*

Even with other German teams receiving more money, Bayern continued to win championship after championship in the Bundesliga. No other team in Germany could do that. In 2013, Bayern won the UEFA Champions League once more. It was Bayern's fifth title, a record that places the team among the best in Europe.

Despite the challenges the club faced during and after World War II, Bayern has become one of the most successful teams in the world. Its youth club's knack for developing local talent like Beckenbauer, Maier, and Müller is its key to success.

A Tradition of Excellence

Bayern players celebrate their victory in the 2005 German Cup.

AWARDS AND CHAMPIONSHIPS

In recent years, Bayern has won many awards and titles for being the best in Germany, Europe, and the world. Few clubs can match their consistency on the field. Year after year, Bayern takes home important titles, beating their rivals and standing out as one of the best clubs in Europe.

LEADING THE BUNDESLIGA

The Bundesliga determines the German soccer champions each year. Each team in the league plays every other team twice. One game is at home, and one is away. Winning a game is worth three points. A draw, or tie, is worth one, and a loss zero. The champions are the team with the most points at the end of the season.

Because of this format, the Bundesliga rewards consistent play. Some tournaments in the United States and Canada can see a team lose their chance of winning with a single loss. A good example is a playoff game in U.S. football. A bad day for one team or a really good day for another can end a team's chances. This is

SPORT SHORT
Between 1960 and 2004, the Intercontinental Cup matched clubs around the world. Bayern Munich won twice.

not the case in the Bundesliga. The winning team is the one that plays the best day in and day out.

Bayern has completely dominated the Bundesliga throughout the league's history, especially in recent years. As of the end of the 2018–2019 season, there had been a total of fifty-six Bundesliga seasons. Bayern placed first in twenty-eight of them—exactly half. This is an amazing accomplishment considering the league today has eighteen teams each season.

In both 2011 and 2012, Borussia Dortmund did manage to take home the title. However, between 2013 and 2018, Bayern won the Bundesliga every year. Borussia Dortmund has placed second in three of those seasons, but they have been unable to defeat Bayern since 2012. One of Bayern's main competitors in Germany today, Borussia Dortmund earns the most money after Bayern, and it has a strong team of German and international stars.

THE GERMAN CUP AND THE GERMAN SUPER CUP

After the Bundesliga, the German Cup is the most sought-after title in German soccer. The German Cup is much less forgiving than the Bundesliga. A single loss eliminates a team from the cup competition. A total of sixty-four teams compete each year. Some are professional, and others are amateurs. The champions must win six games in a row to take home the cup.

Bayern has an outstanding record in the German Cup. From 2010 to 2018, they won the title in 2010, 2013, 2014, and 2016. No other team comes close to winning as often. This number of wins is especially impressive since the winning team must not lose a single game.

The German Super Cup is another important German event. It is a one-off match that pits the Bundesliga champions against the German Cup champions. (When a single team wins both—as Bayern sometimes does—the runner-up of the Bundesliga plays against the winner.)

Since the German Super Cup restarted in 2010 after a break, Bayern has won seven of the nine matches. Bayern lost against Borussia Dortmund in 2012, and in 2011, Bayern did not qualify. In 2018, Bayern won a comfortable 5–0 victory.

Bayern's impressive record in the Bundesliga, the German Cup, and German Super Cup is unmatched by any other German team. Bayern performs well year after year. There is no doubt that they are the top German team today.

The German Super Cup trophy is highly sought after.

Awards and Championships

PROTECTING THE ENVIRONMENT

FC Bayern Munich is committed to protecting the environment. In 2018, Bayern's stadium, Allianz Arena, changed the kind of cups it uses. Instead of disposable cups that end up in landfills, the stadium now uses reusable cups. After each game, the plastic cups are collected and washed.

That same year, Bayern was given an award for this change by the nonprofit organization Environmental Action Germany. One of the organization's leaders made a statement at the opening game of the 2018 season, thanking Bayern:

> Plastic waste has become one of the biggest environmental problems. FC Bayern are therefore showing exactly the right way forward to get this problem under control. The change at the Allianz Arena will save over one million disposable cups over the course of the season. That's why we are presenting the award to FC Bayern. We look forward to other clubs following this positive example.

Bayern's next environmental project is the installation of solar panels on the roof of its parking area. The club aims to produce its own clean energy for Allianz Arena, helping improve its effect on the environment.

THE TREBLE

In soccer, a team is said to complete a treble when it takes home three top trophies in one season. In European soccer, the treble is made up of the national league titles, the national cup titles, and the UEFA Champions League title. Winning all three of these in one year is very difficult. As of 2019, only seven clubs have ever completed the treble in the history of European soccer.

In the 2012–2013 season, Bayern became the first German team to complete the treble after winning the title in the Bundesliga, the German Cup, and the Champions League. It was an outstanding season for Bayern. It cemented the team's place as one of the best in European soccer history.

That season, Bayern won the Bundesliga by a wide margin. They lost just one game. At the end, they had ninety-one points. Borussia Dortmund came in second place with sixty-six points. Bayern and Dortmund qualified for the Champions League as a result.

Both teams then played extraordinarily well in the Champions League and made it to the final game. It was the first time that two German teams battled

The base of the German Cup trophy has the names of past winners written on it.

Awards and Championships 31

for the title of the best club in Europe. The match was close, but as the clock ran down, Bayern scored a goal and won 2–1. It was Bayern's first Champions League title since 2001, and the fifth title in the club's history.

The last match of their 2012–2013 season was the German Cup against VfB Stuttgart. The hardest part—taking home the Champions League title—was over. However, losing the match would have spelled the end of Bayern's dream to complete the treble. Munich took an early lead, and eventually, the score was 3–0. It seemed the treble was guaranteed, until Stuttgart suddenly made a comeback, scoring two goals. With ten minutes left, a Bayern loss seemed possible. Bayern led by just one point. However, Bayern's defense held. They won the German Cup and became the first German team to complete the treble.

SPORT SHORT
Only Real Madrid and AC Milan have won more Champions League titles than Bayern Munich.

BEST PLAYER OF THE YEAR

In 2013, Bayern player Franck Ribéry won the Globe Soccer Award for Best Player of the Year. The Frenchman joined the club in 2007 and was playing for Bayern as a winger when the club completed the treble. Wingers are midfielders who are to the left or right of the center of the field. The midfield is the space between the defense and offense.

Franck Ribéry scores a goal in a Bundesliga match against Werder Bremen in 2007.

Competition was stiff that year, and Ribéry was chosen ahead of two legendary soccer stars, Lionel Messi and Cristiano Ronaldo. Ribéry later told the media that this made the award even more important to him: "It is a special thing to win trophies like this, knowing that you are one of the three nominated players along with Lionel Messi and Cristiano Ronaldo. It is flattering to be alongside those two great players."

While Messi and Ronaldo scored more goals than Ribéry that year, neither could match his winning record. The winger lost just three of fifty-two games in the

Awards and Championships   **33**

BAYERN'S WOMEN'S TEAM

Since 1970, Bayern Munich has also had a women's team. They play in the top German league for women. It is called the Frauen-Bundesliga. Like the men's team, many players are locals from Munich or other parts of Germany, but others are international stars.

The women's team has done quite well in the Bundesliga in recent years. In both 2015 and 2016, they took home the title, earning their place as the best women's team in Germany. In 2012, they won the German Cup for women.

Their toughest opponent is VfL Wolfsburg, which has won numerous Bundesliga and German Cup titles in recent years. Bayern has been one of the few teams able to challenge them at the highest levels of competition in Germany.

Bayern's women's team poses before a 2019 UEFA Women's Champions League game.

season. It was an amazing accomplishment. He also had more assists than either Messi or Ronaldo. In the final match of the UEFA Champions League, it was Ribéry who set up the winning goal in the last minutes of the game with an assist.

THE 2013 FIFA CLUB WORLD CUP

Bayern's victory in the UEFA Champions League qualified the team to play in the FIFA Club World Cup. This is different than the World Cup, where national teams compete against each other. The FIFA Club World Cup tournament is a face-off between the top club teams in the world. In 2013, Bayern was admitted and given the chance to compete outside of Europe and test themselves against new competitors.

Bayern's first match was against Guangzhou Evergrande, a Chinese club. Bayern won 3–0. Ribéry scored the first goal, putting Bayern ahead.

The second game for Bayern was the final match against Raja Casablanca, a Moroccan club. Once again, Bayern did not allow a single goal to go in their net. They managed to score twice against Raja Casablanca. Bayern took home yet another title. They were recognized as the best club in the world in 2013.

Across Germany, FC Bayern Munich fan shops sell clothing, soccer balls, and other items with the club logo.

OVERCOMING CHALLENGES

Bayern Munich's path to victory hasn't always been clear. Like any other club, Bayern has faced big challenges. Some of the challenges are old ones. Others are more modern problems. Many teams have had to deal with financial problems and racism. Bayern Munich is no exception.

MONEY AND SOCCER

While fans might not think of it often, a soccer club's finances play a huge role in its success on the field. Lots of money is needed to pay players their salaries. If a club can't pay talented stars enough money, that club won't be able to bring the best players to the team. Without good players, the team will not play well, and the club's finances can get worse. Lack of money can cause once-great clubs to go from playing on the international stage to playing in a regional league.

Privately owned clubs can sometimes rely on the money of their owner. Some clubs owned by billionaires can spend lots of money to bring in the best players around the world. However, if the club is losing money

SPORT SHORT
Bayern Munich operates shops where fans can buy team merchandise across Germany.

each year, its dominance will last only as long as the attention of its rich owner.

A club that is owned mostly by its fans, like Bayern, needs to make money. If it starts losing money each year, it may have to let some players go in order to survive. Clubs make money a few different ways. On match day, they sell tickets, drinks, and food at their stadium. They also sell the right to show their games on television. Sponsors pay soccer clubs money to promote their brand. The logos of sponsors are shown on player uniforms and in stadiums. Additionally, clubs sell merchandise like soccer balls, mugs, and clothing with the club's logo.

BAYERN AND MONEY

In the 1960s and 1970s, Bayern was having money problems. The club was not selected to join the new Bundesliga in 1963. International stars playing for the team were too expensive. In response, Bayern recruited local talent for little money and trained them to be stars. This plan paid off when Franz Beckenbauer, Gerd Müller, and Sepp Maier helped the team reach the top of European club soccer.

Since that period, Bayern has made making money an important part of its business. Today, the club is one of the most successful in Europe. As of 2019, the club has been profitable for the last twenty-six years. This means it made more money than it spent every year. Such a record is unusual for a club. Many clubs borrow money often and have bad years where they lose lots of games.

As of 2019, Bayern is valued at $3 billion. Only three clubs are valued higher: Manchester United, Real Madrid, and Barcelona. In Germany, Bayern's value and profits are much more than any other club in the Bundesliga.

Bayern has used its wealth to help others. For example, the club has helped German rivals that have been in financial difficulty. In 2004, Bayern gave a loan to Borussia Dortmund—the team that would face off against Bayern in the Champions League final less than a decade later. Bayern president Uli Hoeness spoke to the press about the decision years later when it became public:

> It was a critical situation for Borussia Dortmund. When they couldn't even pay their salaries, we thought we should help. I'm a big fan of tradition in sport, and I think it was the right thing to do.

Bayern also helped its old rival 1860 Munich in 2006. Both teams owned Allianz Arena at the time, but Bayern bought their rival's portion, or share. Despite the sale, 1860 Munich was allowed to keep playing their home games at the massive arena. The agreement only ended in 2017 when 1860 Munich was forced to leave the Bundesliga and play in a smaller regional league.

Overcoming Challenges

OWNED BY ITS FANS

Soccer clubs are big businesses. Like any other business, their ownership can be handled many ways. Extremely rich people own some clubs. For instance, Chelsea FC is owned by billionaire Roman Abramovich. Other clubs are listed on the stock market: anyone with money can buy part of them and share in their profits.

Bayern is owned almost completely by its fans. Fans own 75 percent of the club. This majority allows them to make decisions about the direction of their team. The remaining 25 percent is split between three companies: Audi (a carmaker), Allianz (an insurance company), and Adidas (a sportswear company). All three companies are based in Bavaria.

Fan ownership comes with many perks. Club members feel like they have a real say in how their team operates. Bayern also works hard to keep ticket prices down and maintain an open culture. Fans can often drop in and watch their team practice. Bayern's financial success means that it is likely to remain owned by its fans into the future.

ALLIANZ ARENA

One secret to Bayern's financial success is Allianz Arena. Built between 2002 and 2005, the stadium is a marvel of engineering and architecture. The exterior can light up and can even change colors to match the team playing there: red and white for Bayern or white and blue when 1860 Munich played there. Its impressive appearance from outside has made it one of the most recognizable soccer stadiums in the world.

Allianz Arena also supports the club financially. In addition to ticket and refreshment sales, the stadium itself draws fans and tourists from around the world. There is a museum that traces Bayern Munich's history. It covers its development from a local team to the soccer powerhouse it is today. Fans can also go on stadium tours and see the players' locker rooms and other areas that are usually off-limits. Ticket sales for the museum and tour help support the club and allow it to recruit top players.

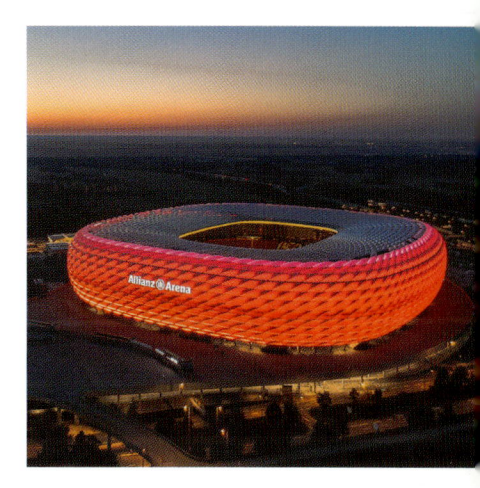

The outer shell of Allianz Arena lights up every evening.

VIOLENCE AND RACISM IN SOCCER

Aside from financial issues, soccer in Europe has faced other big problems. Some of these problems can be traced to the sport's violent past. One of the game's earliest forms took shape in England about a thousand years ago. Crowds of people from neighboring towns would meet and try to kick a pig's bladder through

Overcoming Challenges 41

SPORT SHORT

FC Bayern Munich paid off the loan to build Allianz Arena sixteen years early.

goalposts. The game had few rules. Often, matches became more of a battle than a game. At times, English kings outlawed the early forms of soccer because it was so violent and destructive.

As modern soccer started to develop, more rules were introduced. Battles no longer took place on the field, but some diehard supporters of teams still fought each other. Before, during, and after matches, fans sometimes fought. This rowdy behavior is called "hooliganism." In the 1960s, it became a much-debated issue in Europe, especially in Great Britain. It was called "the British disease," but in truth, violence at soccer matches was a problem across Europe.

Today, soccer leagues try their best to stop violence between fans. However, it can be difficult to stop troublemakers from attending games. Violence is not the only problem that leagues face. Some fans also shout racist abuse at players on the field. Racist abuse distracts and harms players on the field and also makes games an unwelcome place for many people.

Bayern defender Jérôme Boateng has faced the problem of racism in soccer firsthand. In 2013, he was playing for AC Milan when he made headlines for walking off the field during a friendly game due to horrible chants. Since then, he has repeatedly spoken out about the problem of racism in European soccer.

Along with many other players, he feels that leagues are not doing enough to confront the problem.

In 2018, Boateng spoke about trying to make a change. He hoped that soccer authorities in Europe would listen to him, "I had three or four ideas. I put them out there. I spoke to them about it. But at the end of the day, nothing happened. Nothing changed."

Soccer leagues are not the only ones fighting racism. Many individual clubs and players are also tackling the problem. Clubs often ban fans that are caught shouting racist abuse. Teammates also join together on the field to show support for their friends who are targeted.

Bayern Munich player Jérôme Boateng has spoken out about racism in European soccer.

EUROPE'S ULTRAS

It is impossible to talk about violence and racism in soccer without talking about ultras, groups of extremely devoted fans to a specific club. Most European clubs have at least one ultras group, and some have many. Not all ultras are violent or racist, but some groups are. The ultras scene in some countries, like Italy, can be very violent. Rival groups clash in bloody battles in stadiums and on the streets.

Overcoming Challenges 43

In Germany, ultras tend to be less extreme. Violence is rare. Ultras groups usually focus on supporting their team through chanting and choreographed movements, like raising their arms together. Sometimes, they also perform pyrotechnic displays, like waving flares and setting off smoke bombs. These displays are usually against stadium rules due to fire-safety concerns.

Nonetheless, some German ultras have embraced the far right. They look to German history's darkest chapter—Nazism—for inspiration. Since World War II, Nazism has been widely hated in Germany. Most Germans rejected its far-right ideas that discriminated against Jewish people, people of color, foreigners, and LGBT+ people. However, a very small percentage of Germans have embraced its message of hate. Some of these far-right extremists have joined and created ultras groups. There have been incidents of fans shouting Nazi phrases and raising their arms in a Nazi salute.

German clubs try to stop this sort of behavior. When individuals are seen committing racist acts, they are banned from attending games. Other spectators and players on the field also sometimes challenge racist fans. Still, many critics say not enough is being done to protect players who are targets of these actions.

BAYERN'S FIGHT AGAINST EXTREMISM

Bayern has not entirely avoided racism and anti-Semitism. Decades ago, it was possible to see far-right extremism at Bayern matches. However, Bayern's ultras groups took a stand against hatred. They purposefully embraced the club's Jewish past.

Bayern Munich fans display a picture of club president Kurt Landauer to celebrate the club's Jewish roots.

One ultras group, the Schickeria, spearheaded efforts to recognize the club's Jewish president Kurt Landauer. They printed shirts with Landauer's face on them. They hoped that recognition of the club's history would fight discrimination and racism. Eventually, Bayern began to talk about its history more. Before, the club had been mostly silent about the difficult subject of Landauer and the Nazi history of Germany.

Schickeria member Simon Mueller spoke about the campaign to gain recognition for Landauer:

> When I came to the stadiums in the '90s, you had a lot of right-wing people. In Munich, the culture was open to right-wing things. The idea of Kurt Landauer, what he stands for now, is very important. But for me it's important what he means for the people in the stands. It's important for us not to go back to right-wing ideas.

Overcoming Challenges 45

The Schickeria were given the Julius Hirsch Prize in 2014 for their efforts. The prize, named after a German Jewish player who was killed in the Holocaust, recognized the ultras' fight against racism.

Bayern's ultras work hard to make Allianz Arena a place that is safe for everyone. They regularly display banners that condemn racism and other forms of discrimination. The ultras have a reputation for fighting against homophobia, or prejudice against the LGBT+ community. While some ultras and soccer fans across Europe celebrate violence and discrimination, Bayern's fans refuse to support these ideas.

BAYERN AND THE MIGRANT CRISIS

Germany's struggle to contain far-right groups has worsened in recent years. In 2015, a wave of migrants reached Europe. Fleeing violence and poverty in the Middle East and Africa, they asked for asylum, or safety, in Europe. Germany allowed more than a million migrants to stay temporarily while their requests for asylum were heard.

The presence of so many foreigners angered Germany's right-wing extremists. Far-right groups responded with racist abuse and violence. Anti-Semitism also became more common. Although most Germans welcomed the migrants, right-wing extremists became a large and vocal minority.

Bayern Munich decided to take a stand against racism and injustice. The club took steps to help migrants. In 2015, Bayern donated 1 million euros (currency used in Germany), or $1,120,000. The money went to projects that help migrants. The club also set

Bayern players celebrate diversity by bringing some migrant children onto the field before a match on September 12, 2015.

up soccer training camps. Migrants could attend the camps to have fun, learn German, and eat a meal. Bayern CEO Karl-Heinz Rummenigge explained why the club was helping, "Bayern sees it as its social responsibility to help the refugees, needy children, women and men, to help them and to accompany them in Germany."

It was a powerful statement by the most successful sports club in Germany. Despite the racist views of some people, Bayern stood firmly with the migrants. The club used its reputation and example to encourage others to do the same. Bayern, its fans, and its ultras have worked to make sure the club is open and welcoming to everyone.

Bayern players pose for a photograph during a UEFA Champions League match in 2018.

THE FUTURE OF BAYERN

Like all teams, Bayern's future depends on its players. They are the people who will determine whether the club wins titles or not. In the coming years, Bayern will face some unique challenges as it fights to stay the top team in Germany and one of the best teams in Europe. On average, Bayern Munich's players are older than many of its competitors' players. The team needs to bring in new talent to continue to thrive. Bayern's success also means the team struggles to find equally talented teams to play against. This could be a major disadvantage for the club in the future.

SUPREME IN THE BUNDESLIGA

Bayern is a victim of its own success. It is the best team in the Bundesliga. No other German team can beat Bayern often or challenge the team for titles in Germany. On the one hand, this is a key part of Bayern's image. It is why the club is so famous. It is also why Bayern can make enough money to pay for excellent players. On the other hand, it is a serious problem for the team.

Bayern Munich players celebrate after a Bundesliga victory on April 20, 2019.

Since few German teams stand a chance against Bayern, the players get few chances to practice against teams that are their equal. Except for Borussia Dortmund, Bayern is heavily favored going into most matches in the Bundesliga or German Cup. These two competitions make up many of the games that Bayern plays each year. During them, Bayern doesn't get to practice playing against top teams in Europe.

There is little Bayern can do to solve this problem. However, the Bundesliga is looking for ways to improve the quality of other German teams. This situation puts Bayern at a disadvantage compared to other teams in the Champions League. For example, Real Madrid and Barcelona are two Spanish teams that are also some of the best in Europe. Unlike Bayern, they play against each other in La Liga, the Spanish league. The experience and practice of regularly playing against another top team in the world is important.

EXPERIENCED PROS AND NEW BLOOD

All clubs try to find a balance between experienced, older players and younger players who will take over in the future. Both are needed for the long-term success of a club. Bayern's team in the 2018–2019 season was on the older side. The average age was around twenty-six years old.

Many of Bayern's starting players are over the age of thirty. While players this age can still play well on the field, it is necessary to plan for their retirement. In fact, in March 2019, three Bayern players were dropped from the German national team. All three of them were thirty years old. The national team wanted to make room for new, younger players.

MANUEL NEUER

The only player over the age of thirty that the German national team kept is Manuel Neuer. The thirty-three year old is the captain and goalkeeper of both Bayern Munich and the German national team as of 2019. His goalkeeping skills have carried both teams to international success.

In 2013, it was Neuer who stopped shot after shot to help Bayern complete the treble and win the Champions League title. The next year, he

Manuel Neuer blocks a shot during a Champions League match on March 13, 2019.

The Future of Bayern 51

helped the German national team become FIFA World Cup champions.

Each year, the International Federation of Football History and Statistics (IFFHS) picks the best goalkeeper of the season. Between 2013 and 2016, Neuer was picked four times in a row. Around the world, he is considered one of the best goalkeepers of his generation, and he is still a key part of Bayern's success.

ROBERT LEWANDOWSKI

One of Bayern's biggest stars doesn't play on the German national team because he is Polish. Striker Robert Lewandowski turned thirty in August 2018, but he is still at the top of his game. Lewandowski is the captain of the Polish national team and the highest-paid member of Bayern's squad as of 2019. He earns his salary by scoring goal after goal. Since joining the team in 2014, he has been the highest-scoring member of the team in the Bundesliga each year. His contract with Bayern ends in June 2021, but the club will almost surely try to keep him.

Robert Lewandowski was the Bundesliga's top goal scorer in 2018 and 2019.

With stars like Lewandowski and Neuer getting older, Bayern has signed promising young stars. In the future, they will replace the older players.

SPORT SHORT
Manager Niko Kovač was a central midfielder for Bayern Munich between 2001 and 2003.

One of the most recent contracts Bayern signed was for an American teenager from Alabama: Chris Richards.

CHRIS RICHARDS

In 2019, Bayern signed a deal for the young defender that will last until June 2023. The eighteen-year-old American had previously been playing for Bayern on loan from FC Dallas. As of 2019, Chris Richards played for Bayern's youth team. At Allianz Arena, he has learned from some of the best players on the field.

Richards spoke to CBS Sports about his experience in February 2018:

> *The journey has been surreal. The past two to three years, it's been life changing. Going from pretty much a nobody in Alabama to being bought by one of the biggest clubs in the world. The past few months have just been really hectic, but it's been really great for me as a person and a player.*

In addition, the club picked up Canadian winger Alphonso Davies, who was also eighteen when he was signed. The team is hopeful that young international talent will power Bayern far into the future.

American Chris Richards (*left*) is a proud member of Bayern Munich's team.

READY FOR ANYTHING

Over the course of its history, Bayern has proved it's a club ready to handle any challenges it faces. Bayern has established itself as a team on the rise, and its reputation is sure to bring exciting new soccer stars into its ranks. Still, reliable players like Manuel Neuer and Robert Lewandowski continue to show their skill, teamwork, and drive. Bayern's long-term players show the club's values in action. They maintain the tradition, respect, and confidence required to become the best of the Bundesliga.

These values have always held strong. Even in the face of tragedy, the club has survived. Bayern was able to make it through the most terrible chapter of German history, the Holocaust. As a team with proud Jewish roots, this is remarkable. The story of FC Bayern Munich and its dominance is about more than just soccer. It is proof that people can go through the worst and come out on top.

CHRONOLOGY

1900 FC Bayern Munich is founded by seventeen players at a local restaurant.

1926 Bayern wins the South German Championship for the first time.

1932 Bayern wins its first German soccer championship and is recognized as the best team in Germany that year.

1933 Jewish club president Kurt Landauer steps down as anti-Semitism in Germany builds.

1939 Nazi Germany invades Poland, beginning World War II and the Holocaust.

1947 Two years after the end of World War II, Kurt Landauer once again becomes president of FC Bayern Munich.

1962 The Bundesliga is formed, but Bayern is passed over in favor of 1860 Munich.

1968 Bayern wins its first Bundesliga title.

1976 Bayern wins the Champions League title for the third year in a row.

2004 Bayern gives a loan to rival German team Borussia Dortmund when they experience financial troubles.

2005 Allianz Arena opens. Bayern Munich and 1860 Munich begin playing their home games there.

2013 Bayern completes the treble, winning the Champions League, Bundesliga, and German Cup.

2014 A group of Bayern ultras are given the Julius Hirsch Prize for their fight against anti-Semitism and prejudice.

2015 The European migrant crisis begins, and Bayern donates money to help people arriving in Germany.

2019 Eighteen-year-old American Chris Richards signs a deal with Bayern.

GLOSSARY

anti-Semitism Prejudice toward Jewish people; anti-Semitism was built into laws during the Nazi era of Germany.

assist In soccer, a play that happens when someone passes the ball to another player who then scores a goal.

Bundesliga The national soccer league of Germany that sees the top eighteen teams face off.

Champions League A soccer competition that pits the best thirty-two clubs across Europe against each other.

club A team.

condemn To speak out against something.

German Cup A tournament between the sixty-four best German teams.

far right A group of individuals who have very conservative beliefs that often include racism and anti-Semitism.

financial Relating to money.

flattering Pleasing.

formalize To make something official.

hectic Very busy or fast-paced.

Holocaust The murder of six million European Jewish people and millions of others by Nazi Germany between 1939 and 1945.

league A group of soccer teams that compete with each other for trophies and other soccer awards every year.

prestigious Well-respected.

right-wing extremists Very conservative people who oppose immigration and minority groups. In Germany, anti-Semitism and opposition to Islam are common among right-wing extremists.

treble In soccer, an achievement that is completed when a team wins the title for their national league, national cup, and the European-wide Champions League.

ultras Soccer fans who are especially dedicated to their team.

FURTHER INFORMATION

BOOKS

Herman, Gail, and Jerry Hoare. *What Was the Holocaust?* New York, NY: Penguin, 2018.

Jökulsson, Illugi. *Stars of World Soccer*. Second edition. New York, NY: Abbeville Press, 2018.

Whiting, Jim. *Bayern Munich*. Soccer Champions. Mankato, MN: The Creative Company, 2016.

Williams, Heather. *FC Bayern Munich*. Inside Professional Soccer. Calgary, Canada: Weigl Educational Publishers, 2018.

WEBSITES

Bayern Munich

https://www.transfermarkt.com/fc-bayern-munchen/startseite/verein/27

Explore the latest stats, squad lineup, and much more on this website.

Bundesliga

https://bundesliga.com/en/bundesliga

The Bundesliga's official website gives fans the latest scores, match schedules, and articles about Bundesliga clubs.

Germany

https://kids.nationalgeographic.com/explore/countries/germany

Read interesting facts and look at photos and maps on *National Geographic Kids*' webpage about Germany.

Our Values

https://fcbayern.com/en/club/values

Learn more about the values that guide FC Bayern Munich on the club's official website.

VIDEOS

Allianz Arena (Munich, Germany) Time Lapse | panTerra

https://www.youtube.com/watch?v=QdXCLnmLeFo

Watch the Allianz Arena being built.

Bayern v. Dortmund: 2013 UEFA Champions League Final Highlights

https://www.youtube.com/watch?v=wA4ChhQ38GQ

This short video shows Bayern winning the 2013 UEFA Champions League title match.

A Day with Chris Richards at FC Bayern Campus

https://www.youtube.com/watch?v=yNuwExbCywc

Chris Richards gives viewers a full tour of the FC Bayern campus, where the youth league lives, trains, and plays.

Further Information

SELECTED BIBLIOGRAPHY

Bundesliga. "The Cat from Anzing." Accessed March 1, 2019. https://www.bundesliga.com/en/news/Bundesliga/0000243142.jsp.

Gonzalez, Roger. "Bayern Munich's Rising Prospect Chris Richards Is Setting His Sights on Becoming a Household Name for American Soccer." CBS Sports, February 15, 2019. https://www.cbssports.com/soccer/news/bayern-munichs-rising-prospect-chris-richards-is-setting-his-sights-on-becoming-an-household-name-for-american-soccer.

Iredahl, Marcus. "From the Südkurve with Love: The Vocal World of the Bundesliga's Ultras." SB Nation, February 14, 2019. https://www.bavarianfootballworks.com/2019/2/14/18219333/bayern-munich-sudkurve-dortmund-yellow-wall-bundesliga-schickeria-fan-protest-dfb-chemnitz.

Liew, Jonathan. "Bayern Munich v. Real Madrid: Champions League's Greatest Rivalry." *Telegraph*, April 29, 2014. https://www.telegraph.co.uk/sport/football/competitions/champions-league/10783424/Bayern-Munich-v-Real-Madrid-Champions-Leagues-greatest-rivalry.html.

Lovell, Mark. "Bayern Munich Cancel Allianz Arena Contract with 1860 Munich." ESPN, July 12, 2017. http://www.espn.com/soccer/tsv-1860-munich/story/3156509/bayern-munich-cancel-allianz-arena-contract-with-1860-munich.

"Migrants Applauded by 75,000 Fans at German Soccer Game." *Times of Israel*, September 12, 2015. https://www.timesofisrael.com/migrants-applauded-by-75000-fans-at-bundesliga-game.

Nelson, Rosa. "Franz Beckenbauer." FootballHistory.org. Accessed March 1, 2019. https://www.footballhistory.org/player/franz-beckenbauer.html.

Rodriguez, Alfredo. "Ribery Is Crowned UEFA Best Player in Europe." UEFA, August 29, 2013. https://www.uefa.com/insideuefa/uefa-best-player-award/news/newsid=1987374.html.

Shankar, Alankrith. "Rivals: Bayern Munich vs. 1860 Munich | The Munich Derby." Outside of the Boot. Accessed March 1, 2019. http://outsideoftheboot.com/2017/05/01/rivals-bayern-munich-vs-1860-munich-the-munich-derby.

Sherman, Kevin. "Bayern Munich, Kurt Landauer, and a Defiance of the Nazis." *These Football Times*, July 9, 2017. https://thesefootballtimes.co/2017/09/07/bayern-munich-kurt-landauer-and-a-defiance-of-the-nazis.

Simpson, Kevin E. *Soccer Under the Swastika: Stories of Survival and Resistance During the Holocaust*. Lanham, MD: Rowman and Littlefield, 2016.

Taylor, Daniel. "It Is Only Nine Years Since Bayern Munich Bailed Out Dortmund with €2M." *Guardian*, May 2, 2013. https://www.theguardian.com/football/2013/may/02/bayern-munich-dortmund-champions-league.

Wahl, Grant. "Inside the SuperClubs: Bayern Great Beckenbauer Recalls Time in the USA." *Sports Illustrated*, November 17, 2014. https://www.si.com/soccer/planet-futbol/2014/11/17/bayern-munich-franz-beckenbauer-inside-superclubs-nasl-cosmos.

Whitney, Clark. "Five Amazing Franck Ribery Stats No One Talks About." *Bleacher Report*, January 27, 2015. https://bleacherreport.com/articles/2340860-5-amazing-franck-ribery-stats-no-one-talks-about#slide1.

"Who Are the Best Big-Game Goalscorers in Football History?" *Guardian*. Accessed March 1, 2019. https://www.theguardian.com/football/blog/2013/feb/06/best-big-game-goalscorer-football-history.

INDEX

Page numbers in **boldface** are images.

1860 Munich, 15, 20, 39, 41

Allianz Arena, 30, 39, 41–42, **41**, 46, 53
anti-Semitism, 11, 16, 19, 44, 46
assist, 35

Barcelona, 39, 50
Bavaria, 14, **14**, 16, 20, 22, 40
Beckenbauer, Franz, 20–25, **22**, 38
Borussia Dortmund, 9, 28–29, 31, 39, 50
Bundesliga, 7–9, 15, 19–20, 23–25, 27–29, 31, 34, 38–39, 49–50, 52, 54

Champions League, 8–9, 23–25, 31–32, 35, 39, 50–51
club, 5–11, 13–14, 16, 18, 20–25, 27–28, 30–32, 35, 37–41, 43–47, 49, 51–54

concentration camps, 17–18
condemn, 46

defender, 20, 42, 53

East Germany, 19–20
European Champions Clubs' Cup, 8, **8**

far right, 44, 46
FC Nürnberg, 14
FIFA Club World Cup, **9**, 35
financial, 10, 37, 39–41
flattering, 33
formalize, 5

German Cup, 19, **26**, 28–29, 31–32, **31**, 34, 50

hectic, 53
Hitler, Adolf, 11, 16
Holocaust, the, 17–18, 46, 54
hooliganism, 42

Landauer, Kurt, 16–18, **17**, 45, **45**

62 FC Bayern Munich

league, 5, 7, 13, 15, 19–20, 23, 27–28, 31, 34, 37, 39, 42–43, 50
logo, **7**, **36**, 38

Maier, Sepp, 20, 22–23, **22**, 25, 35
Messi, Lionel, 22, 33, 35
midfield, 32, 35
migrants, 46–47, **47**
Müller, Gerd, **12**, 20, 22–23, **22**, 25, 38

Nazi party, 11, 16–19, 44–45
Neuer, Manuel, **4**, 51–52, **51**, 54

prestigious, 8

racism, 11, 37, 41–46
Real Madrid, 8, 32, 39, 50

Ribéry, Franck, 32–33, **33**, 35
Richards, Chris, 53, **54**
right-wing extremists, 45–46
Ronaldo, Cristiano, 33, 35

sponsors, 38
sweeper, 20

thrive, 49, 54
treble, 31–32, 51

ultras, 43–47
Union of European Football Association (UEFA), 8

West Germany, 19–21
winger, 32–33, 53
World Cup, 9–10, 21, 24, 35
World War II, 25, 44

Index 63

ABOUT THE AUTHOR

Derek Miller is a writer and educator from Salisbury, Maryland. He has written dozens of books for students, including *Science Investigators: Investigating Energy Through Modeling* and *How Government Works: Collecting Taxes*. When he's not reading, writing, or researching, Miller likes to travel with his wife and root for FC Bayern Munich.